# Irish Wisdom:

## A Book of Quotations

# *Irish Wisdom:*

## A Book of Quotations

Edited by Tom Slattery

**BARNES**
**& NOBLE**
**BOOKS**
NEW YORK

Compilation copyright © 2004 by Barnes & Noble, Inc.

2004 Barnes & Noble Books

ISBN 0-7607-6108-6

Printed and bound in the United States of America

04 05 06 07 08 HC 9 8 7 6 5 4 3 2 1

*They're [Ireland] a verbal nation, partly because
a nation on the run couldn't be chipping away
at stone or painting, and partly because
it is the Celtic tradition.*
—TIM PAT COOGAN, interview, April 16, 2000

IF I HAVE LEARNED ANYTHING IN MY TWENTY YEAR ROMP
into my Irish heritage, it is how lucky the English
language has been to have the Irish give it their
stamp of approval; and an elegant stamp it is.

As a tour guide to the Emerald Isle for the past
ten years and as the president of a nonprofit associ-
ation in the process of building a Celtic collection,
I have fallen under the spell of not only the great
writers, but also the everyday speaker. Yes, as the
saying goes, "The Irish do have a way with words."
And this explains my delight in the opportunity to
delve into this phenomenon by selecting a sampling
for you readers. Be assured, this is but a mere taste
of the magnificent banquet that is "Irish Wisdom."

Lest you think I exaggerate, this small country
already has four Nobel Prize Laureates in Literature,
and this in a language relatively new to their country.

The history of the great civilizations of Eire was first passed down by the storytellers of old, then copied by the learned monks into various languages—the last of which was Gaelic, the present national language. As late as the mid-nineteenth century, Gaelic was still the predominant language of the common folk. In fact, most of the proverbs used here are translations of the original.

And it be not only the literary figure that has contributed to the richness of his or her new language. You need only to read an Irish or Irish American newspaper, listen to an Irish sports event or newscast, or simply eavesdrop on a conversation to realize how the Gael has contributed. The accent is pleasant, but it is in the turn of the phrase that one notices the wit, the cynicism, the barb so smooth and cutting that one caresses one's body to feel where the knife entered. Yes, this linguistic ability is a true demonstration of "Irish Wisdom."

—*Tom Slattery*

# Proverbs 101

*It is more difficult to maintain honor than to become prosperous.*

*Everyone is wise until he speaks.*

*You'll never plow a field by turning it over in your mind.*

*Soft words butter no parsnips but they won't harden the heart of the cabbage either.*

*If you lie down with dogs you'll rise with fleas.*

*It's no use carrying an umbrella if your shoes are leaky.*

*A trout in the pot is better than a salmon in the sea.*

*If you put a silk dress on a goat he is a goat still.*

*He knows the price of everything and the value of nothing.*

*What's the world to a man whose wife is a widow?*

*A little dog can start a hare, but it takes a big one to catch it.*

*As honest as the cat when the meat is out of reach.*

*You are not a full fledged sailor until you have sailed under full sail, and you have not built a wall unless you rounded a corner.*

*Praise the young and they will blossom.*

*Both your friend and your enemy think that you will never die.*

*Two shorten the road.*

*Listen to the sound of the river and you will get
a trout.*

*May you be in heaven a half hour before the devil
knows you're dead.*

*When you reach the inn of death I hope it's closing
time.*

*May the lips that say ill of you never say thanks
to St. Peter.*

—OLD SAYING

*May the roof above never fall in, and may those
within never fall out.*

*Show the fatted calf, but not the thing that
fattened him.*

*A windy day is not the day for thatching.*

*Three kinds of men who fail to understand women;
young men, old men, and middle-aged men.*

# A Wee Bit of Irish Poetry and Verse

Present day Irish poets are believers—heretical believers, maybe—but they have the spiritual buoyancy of a belief in something. The sort of belief I see in Ireland is a belief emanating from life, from nature, from revealed religion, and from the nation. A sort of dream that produces a sense of magic; indeed there are few signs of the awful sense of respect for words which poetry demands.

—F. R. HIGGINS (1896-1941),
*Tendencies in Modern Poetry*

But I have no spade to follow men like them
Between my finger and my thumb
The squat pen rests.
I'll dig with it.

—SEAMUS HEANEY (1939- ), "Digging"

But sooner a wonder came to light,
That showed the rogues they lied;
The man recovered of the bite,
The dog it was that died.

—OLIVER GOLDSMITH (1728-1774),
"Elegy on the Death of a Mad Dog"

But I being poor, have only my dreams;
I have spread my dreams under your feet;
Tread softly because you tread on my dreams.

—WILLIAM BUTLER YEATS (1865-1939),
"He Wishes for the Clothes of Heaven"

The lying man has promised
Whatever things he could
The greedy man believes him
And thinks his promise good.

—OLD IRISH RANN (quatrain)

The man who only took
His learning from a book
If that from him is took
He knows not where to look.

—OLD IRISH RANN (quatrain)

As a white candle / in a holy place
So is the beauty / of an aged face.

—JOSEPH CAMPBELL (1879-1944),
"The Old Woman"

This lovely land that always sent
Her writers and artists to banishment
And in the spirit of Irish fun,
Betrayed her leaders, one by one.

—JAMES JOYCE (1882–1941), "Gas from a Burner"

The world's more full of weeping
than we can understand.

—WILLIAM BUTLER YEATS (1865–1939),
"The Stolen Child"

Be green upon their graves, O happy Spring!
For they are young and eager who are dead.

—JAMES STEPHENS (1880–1950), "Spring"

We are the music makers,
We are the dreamers of dreams.

—ARTHUR O'SHAUGHNESSY (1844–1881), "Ode"

I am Ireland: I am older than the Old Woman
   of Beare
Great is my story; I have born Cuchulainn the
   valiant.
Great is my shame; my own children that sold
   their mother.
I am Ireland; I am lonelier than the Old Woman
   of Beare.

—"MISE EIRE," translated by Padraic Pearse
(1879-1916)

I will arise and go now, and go to Inisfree
And a small cabin build there, of clay and
   waddles made.
Nine bean-rows will I have there, and a hive for
   the honey-bee
And live alone in the bee-loud glade.

—WILLIAM BUTLER YEATS, "Inisfree"

Up the airy mountains / Down the rushy glen
We daren't go a-hunting / for fear of little men
Wee folk, good folk / trooping all together;
Green jacket, red cap / and white owl's feather.

—WILLIAM ALLINGHAM (1824–1889), "Fairies"

He gave the little Wealth he had
To build a House for Fools and Mad;
And shew'd by one satiric touch
No Nation wanted it so much.

—VERSE ON JONATHON SWIFT (1667–1745)
endowing a mental hospital

When you are old and gray and full of sleep
And nodding by the fire, take down this book
And slowing read, and dream of the soft look
Your eyes had once, and of their shadows deep.

—W. B. YEATS, "When You are Old"

That Norman, Ken and Sidney signaled Prod
And Seamus (call me Sean) was sure-fire Pape
O land of password, handgrip, wink and nod,
Of open mind as open as a trap . . .

 —SEAMUS HEANEY, "Whatever You Say Say Nothing"

Rise up and plant your feet as men
Where now you crawl like slaves
And make the harvest fields your camp,
Or make them your graves.

 —FANNY PARNELL, verse on the land question (1870's)

The Banshee mournful wails
In the midst of the silent, lonely night
Plaintive she sings the song of death.

       —AN ANCIENT BARD

When food is scarce / And your larder's bare /
And no rashers grease your pan
When hunger grows / As your meals grow rare /
A pint of plain is your only man.

—FLANN O'BRIEN (1911–1966)

There is in every cook's opinion / no savoury
    dish without an onion
But lest your kissing should be spoiled / The
    onion must be thoroughly boiled.

—JONATHON SWIFT

Irish poetry remains a creation happily, funda-
mentally rooted in the rural civilization, yet aware
and in touch with the elements of the future.

—F. R. HIGGINS, *Tendencies in Modern Poetry*

# The Quotables: Wilde & Shaw

Don't let your tongue cut your throat.

—PROVERB

Fashion is a form of ugliness so intolerable that we have to alter it every six months.

—OSCAR WILDE (1854-1900)

You see things, and you say, "Why?" But I dream things that never were, and I say "why not?"

—George Bernard Shaw (1856-1950)

Who, being loved, is poor?

—Oscar Wilde

The power of accurate observation is commonly called cynicism by those who have not got it.

—George Bernard Shaw

A man can't be too careful in his choice of enemies.

—Oscar Wilde

Progress is impossible without change, and those who cannot change their mind cannot change anything.

—George Bernard Shaw

Some cause happiness wherever they go, others, whenever they go.

—OSCAR WILDE

A government that robs Peter to pay Paul, can always depend on the support of Paul.

—GEORGE BERNARD SHAW

We are all in the gutter, but some of us are looking at the stars.

—OSCAR WILDE

I often quote myself, it adds spice to my conversation.

—GEORGE BERNARD SHAW

The difference between literature and journalism is that journalism is unreadable and literature is unread.

—O<small>SCAR</small> W<small>ILDE</small>

I could not write the words Mr. Joyce uses: my prudish hands would refuse to form the letters.

—G<small>EORGE</small> B<small>ERNARD</small> S<small>HAW</small>

Well, he hasn't become important enough to have any enemies. But none of his friends like him.

—O<small>SCAR</small> W<small>ILDE</small>, commenting on young<br>George Bernard Shaw

England had conquered Ireland, so there was nothing for it but to come over and conquer England, which you will notice I have done pretty thoroughly; one way or the other, my Dear, we Irish will prevail.

—George Bernard Shaw

Don't give a woman advice. One should never give a woman anything she can't wear in the evening.

—Oscar Wilde

Americans adore me and will go on adoring me until I say something nice about them.

—George Bernard Shaw

I never travel without my diary; one should always have something sensational to read on the train.

—OSCAR WILDE

I'd rather be an Irishman than an Englishman, but then, who wouldn't?

—GEORGE BERNARD SHAW

"Was the play well received?" asked Whistler (the famous Irish-American painter).
"Oh, the play itself was a huge success, but the audience was a total failure" replied Wilde.

If one could only teach the English how to talk, and the Irish how to listen, society would be quite civilized.

—OSCAR WILDE

The only thing to do with good advice is to pass it on. It is never of any use for oneself.

—Oscar Wilde

The Irish forgive their great men when they are safely buried.

—Proverb

# Other Notable Quotables

St. Patrick's Day is an enchanted time—a day to begin transforming winter's dreams into summer's magic.

—ADRIENNE COOK

There is no language like the Irish for soothing and quieting.

—JOHN MILLINGTON SYNGE (1871–1909)

21

The only factor becoming scarce in a world of abundance is human attention.

—KEVIN KELLY (1952- ), *Wired* magazine

Ireland is a fruitful mother of genius, but a barren nurse.

—JOHN BOYLE O'REILLY (1844-1890)

The Irish have got the gab but are too touchy to be humorous. Me too.

—EDNA O'BRIEN (1932- )

Remember me is all I ask, yet the remembrance prove a task, Forget.

—PERCY FRENCH (1854-1920)

You write like an Irishman. You don't write like an American.

—SEAN O'CASEY (1880-1964) to Eugene O'Neill

Nothing in Ireland lasts long except the miles.

—GEORGE MOORE (1852-1933)

Politics is the chloroform of the Irish people, or rather the hashish.

—OLIVER ST. JOHN GOGARTY (1878-1957)

You have disgraced yourself again.

—W. B. YEATS to unruly audience attending
*The Plough and the Stars*

They are all gone now, and there isn't anything more the sea can do to me.

—JOHN MILLINGTON SYNGE, *Riders to the Sea*

If I knew who Godot was I would have said so.

—SAMUEL BECKETT (1906–1989), author of *Waiting for Godot*

A wise man should have money in his head but not in his heart.

—JONATHON SWIFT

Women are wiser than men because they know less and understand more.

—JAMES STEPHENS, *Crock of Gold*

Nothing is funnier than unhappiness.

—SAMUEL BECKETT, *Endgame*

Satire is sort of glass, wherein beholders do generally discover everybody's facebut their own.

—JONATHON SWIFT

The whole world's in a terrible state of chassis.

—SEAN O'CASEY, *Juno and the Paycock*

This is one race of people for whom psychoanalysis is of no use whatsoever.

—SIGMUND FREUD (1856–1939), on the Irish

When I came back to Dublin I was court-martialed in my absence and sentenced to death in my absence, so I told them they could shoot me in my absence.

—Brendan Behan (1923-1964)

The cup of Ireland's misfortunes has been overflowing for centuries, and it is not full yet.

—Sir Boyle Roche (1743-1807)

Everywhere I go I'm asked if I think the universities stifle writers. My opinion is that they do not stifle enough of them.

—Flannery O'Brien (1911-1966)

# Even More Literary Quoters & Versers

I am a drinker with writing problems.

—BRENDAN BEHAN

If it were raining soup, the Irish would go out with forks.

—BRENDAN BEHAN

There is no such thing as bad publicity, except your own obituary.

—BRENDAN BEHAN

All the world is a stage and most of us are desperately unrehearsed.

—SEAN O'CASEY (1880-1964)

Behind Ireland fierce and militant, is Ireland poetic, passionate, remembering, idyllic, fanciful, and always patriotic.

—W. B. YEATS,
"Popular Ballad Poetry of Ireland," 1897 review

My intention was to write a chapter of the moral history of my country and I chose Dublin for the scene because that city seemed to me the center of paralysis.

—JAMES JOYCE (1882-1941),
letter to Grant Richards, 1905

No true Irishman sees a distinction between the battlefield and the scaffold. Both are fields of honor for our race.

—CANON PATRICK AUGUSTINE SHEEHAN (1852-1913),
*The Graves at Kilmorna*

We need not feel the bitterness of the past to discover its meaning for the present and the future.

—W. B. YEATS

Did they dare, did they dare to slay Owen Roe
  O'Neill?
Yes, they slew with poison him they feared to
  meet with steel.

—THOMAS DAVIS (1814-1845)

Human Blood is no cement for the temple of liberty.

—DANIEL O'CONNELL (1775-1847)

Here I feel permanence as I look at the territory of my people around the foot of Erigal where they've settled.

—CATHAL O'SEARCAIGH (1956- )

You may break, you may ruin the vase, if you will but the scent of the roses will hang around still.

—THOMAS MOORE (1779-1852), "Farewell"

The sniper turned over the dead body and looked into his brother's face.

—LIAM O'FLAHERTY (1896-1984), "The Sniper"

It's among the many misfortunes of Ireland that she has never yet produced a great poet.

—JOHN O'LEARY (1830-1907),
February 1886 lecture

We have just enough religion to make us hate but not enough to make us love one another.

—JONATHON SWIFT, "Thoughts on Various Subjects"

The wind is wild tonight, there's battle in the air
The wind is from the west, and it seems to blow
    from Clare...

—EMILY LAWLESS (1845-1913)

The man who is not afraid of the sea will soon be drownded, for he will be going out on a day he shouldn't. But we do be afraid of the sea and we only do be drownded now and again.

—JOHN MILLINGTON SYNGE,
"Playboy of the Western World"

Oh my grief, I've lost him surely. I've lost the only Playboy of the Western World.

—John Millington Synge,
"Playboy of the Western World"

As soon as the kettle boils, we'll wet a mouthful of tea and discuss your business.

—John B. Keane (1928-2002), "Guaranteed Pure"

At a time when the social reformer was being denounced as a Red and an anticleric, the writer quietly took over and wrote beautifully of birth and death and love in one of the remotest parts of Europe.

—Brian Friel (1929- ), on writer/revolutionary
Peader O'Connell

# Irish History
# With a Bit of
# Mythology

To every cow its calf—to every book its copy.

—KING DIARMAIT's judgement in 561 against
Columcille (521–597)

I'll tell you this, early this morning I signed my death warrant.

—MICHAEL COLLINS (1870–1922), on signing the
Treaty with Great Britain in 1921

I vow that the eyes of justice, the eyes of this journalist will not be shut again.

—VERONICA GUERIN (1959-1996),
on release from hospital after beating in 1995

There was no famine. There can be no famine in a country overflowing with food.

—JOHN MITCHEL (1815-1875), 1861 speech

Let us not dare to forget the terrible death and suffering that occurred between 1845 and In fact we should indelibly fix it in our personal and collective memory for we are our ancestors.

—JANE WILDE (1826-1896), mother of Oscar Wilde

No political change whatsoever is worth the shedding of a single drop of human blood.

—DANIEL O'CONNELL (1775-1847)

Why should Ireland be treated as a geographical fragment of England.... Ireland is not a geographical fragment, but a nation.

—CHARLES STEWART PARNELL (1846–1891),
1875 speech

No longer shall our children, like cattle, be brought up for export.

—EAMON DE VALERA (1882–1975), 1934 speech

Nothing can exceed the deplorable state of this place.

—FAMINE RELIEF OFFICIAL IN SKIBBEREEN,
County Cork in late 1840's

The worker is the slave of the capitalist society, the female worker is the slave of that slave.

—JAMES CONNOLLY (1868–1916),
"The Conquest of Ireland," 1915

We were sent out to make some compromise, bargain or arrangement; we made an arrangement; the arrangement is not satisfactory to many people. Let them criticize on that point, but do not let them say that we were sent out to get one thing and that we got something else.

—ARTHUR GRIFFITH (1872-1922),
1921 debate on the Treaty

I know more after six and a half years of being President about real human rights, human endeavour, human aspirations, poverty and deprivation. It's because I have had to forget the tools of doing and learn the skills of listening and the linking.

—MARY ROBINSON (1944- ),
UN High Commissioner for Human Rights
(1997-2002)

The noblest share of earth is the far western
world
Whose name is written Scotia in the ancient
books.

—Donatus (9th century),
Irish-born Bishop of Fiesole (Italy)

From the fury of the O'Flaherties, the Good Lord
deliver us.

—Inscription on the West Gate in Galway

Neither 'O' nor 'Mac' shall strutted ne swaggere
thro the streets of Galway.

—1518 law passed in Galway

I am Patrick, a sinner, the least learned of men, least of all the faithful, most worthless in the eyes of many.

—St. Patrick (387-493), *Confessions*

Ireland is extremely unique and privileged to have preserved as part of her heritage a large body of ancient law tracts, known collectively as "Fenechas," the law of the Feine (Freemen), or more commonly, the Brehon Law.

—L. MacDonald, *Dalriada Magazine*, 1993

Welcome warriors, to you who have come from afar, this island shall henceforth belong and from the setting to the rising sun there is no better land. And you will be the most perfect the world has ever seen.

—DeDannan goddess, Eire, welcoming the Milesians (circa 1000 BC.)

In truth, neither of you is better or nobler than the other, but I will go with you, Manannon, for you have no other mate worthy of you, but Cuchulainn has Emer.

—FAND (Pearl of Beauty) to her husband,
Manannon, the sea god

I, who have written down this story or, rather, fantasy, don't believe a word of it. It is filled with wicked lies and poetical fantasies. Some bits are possible, others not. Most are just for the entertainment of idiots.

—MONKISH SCRIBE AFTER COPYING THE *TAIN*

I will never be satisfied as long as the meanest cottager in Ireland has a link of the British chain clanking to his rags....

—HENRY GRATTAN (1746–1820), at the inauguration
of the 1782 Irish Parliament

It is my considered opinion that in the fullness of time, history will record the greatness of Collins and it will be recorded at my expense.

—EAMON DE VALERA

I have never and never will accept the right of a minority who happens to be a majority in a small part of the country to opt out of a nation.

—JACK LYNCH, *Irish Times*, November 14, 1970

# Northern Ireland and England

Suddenly as the riot squad moved in, it raining exclamation marks, nuts, bolts, nails, car keys...

—Ciaran Carson (1948– ), "Belfast Confetti"

They have shown us what ordinary people can do to promote peace. They took the first step. They did so in the name of humanity and love of their neighbor; someone had to start forgiving...

—Egil Aarvik presenting the 1977 Nobel Peace Prize to Betty Williams and Mairead Corrigan

A Celt will soon be as rare on the banks of the Shannon as a red man on the banks of Manhattan.

–*LONDON TIMES* editorialist, 1848

... there's no timber to hang a man, no water to drown a man, nor no earth to bury a man.

—ONE OF CROMWELL'S OFFICERS reporting on the Burren, 1649

It has pleased God to bless our endeavours at Drogheda.

—OLIVER CROMWELL (1599-1658), 1649

The sense of frustration which I felt under the tight and immovable Unionist regime became distasteful.

—Playwright BRIAN FRIEL on why he left Derry

I want to see an Ireland of partnership where we wage war on want and poverty, where we reach out to the marginalised and dispossessed, where we build together a future that can be as great as our dreams allow.

—JOHN HUME (1937- ), 1998 Nobel Peace Prize acceptance speech

Ulster will fight and Ulster will be right.

—LORD RANDOLPH CHURCHILL (1849-1895), 1886

Yes, Ulster has many obstacles to overcome of late, but its most serious problems are still January and February.

—PATRICK IRELAND (1935- )

We must be prepared, the morning Home Rule passes, ourselves to become responsible for the government of the Protestant province of Ulster.

—Quoted in Lyons, "Ireland Since the Fenians"

For half a century, it (Unionist party Government) has misgoverned us. Now we are witnessing its dying convulsion, and with traditional Irish mercy, when we got it done, we will kick it into the ground.

—Bernadette Devlin (1947- )

I have always said that I am an Orangeman first and politician afterwards; all I boast is that we are a Protestant Parliament for a Protestant State.

—James Craig (1871-1940)

There you have a starving population, an absentee aristocracy, and an alien Church, and in addition the weakest executive in the world. That is the Irish question.

—BENJAMIN DISRAELI (1804-1881),
House of Commons speech, February 16, 1844

The truth is that Ulster Unionists are not loyal to the crown, but the half-crown.

—JOHN HUME, *The Irish Times*,
"This Week They Said," August 23, 1969

Me? I'm trying to find time to take swimming lessons. If the peace boat hits a rock it might be useful.

—GERRY ADAMS (1948- ), *The Quest for Peace*

Many in the audience employ Catholics, but I do not have one about my place.

Poor Croppies, ye know your sentence has
    come,
When you heard the dread sound of the
    Protestant drum.
In memory of William we hoisted the flag
And soon the bright Orange put down the
    Green rag.

—From "Croppies Lie Down"

I went home after the march that weekend, home to my own community, and all I can say, the only way I can describe it is that the mask came down....

—Inez McCormick, about the ambush of peace marchers at Burntollet Bridge, 1969

Being born in a stable does not make one a horse....

—DUKE OF WELLINGTON, born in Dublin
(1769-1852), in denying his Irish citizenship

I have tried to break the chains of ancient hatreds. I have been unable to realize during my period of office all that I sought to achieve. Whether now it can be achieved in my life-time I do not know, But one day these things will be and must be achieved.

—TERENCE O'NEILL (1914-1990), resignation as
NI Premier, television speech April 18, 1969

The Catholics have been interfering in Ulster affairs since 1641.

—IAN PAISLEY (1926- ), *The Irish Times*,
"This Week They Said," August 30, 1969

The three components of Unionism are British heritage, Protestantism and supremacy. British heritage and Protestantism they should have, a man is entitled to his heritage, but supremacy they cannot have, any more than the Boer can in South Africa.

—Tim Pat Coogan (1935- ), interview,
*The Irish-Australian Newspaper*, 1996

If Gladstone goes for Home Rule, the Orange card would be the only one to play. Please God it will turn out the ace of trump and not the two.

—Randolph Churchill, letter to a friend, 1886

Lloyd George, Britain's PM allegedly said,
  "Arguing with de Valera is like trying to
  pick up mercury with a fork."
de Valera's reply: "Why doesn't he use a spoon?"

—pre-Treaty negotiations, summer of 1921

# Irish
# Nationalism

BRITISH OFFICER: "You're seven minutes late,
  Mr. Collins."
MICHAEL COLLINS: "You've kept us waiting 700
  years. You can have your seven minutes."
  —CEREMONY TO TAKE DOWN THE BRITISH FLAG in 1922

The odds are a thousand to one against us, but
in the event of victory, hold on to your rifles, as
those with whom we are fighting may stop before
our goal is reached.

—JAMES CONNELLY, to his Citizen Army in 1916

49

... but the fools, the fools, the fools!—they have left us our Fenian dead, and while Ireland holds these graves, Ireland unfree shall never be at peace.

—PADRAIC PEARSE, at O'Donovan Ross's funeral, 1915

The great appear great because we are on our knees; let us arise.

—JAMES CONNOLLY, 1896

To gain what is worth having, it may be necessary to lose everything.

—BERNADETTE DEVLIN MCALISKEY

Yesterday I dared to struggle. Today I dare to win.

—BERNADETTE DEVLIN MCALISKEY

There is no crime in detecting and destroying in war-time, the spy and the informer. They have destroyed without trial. I have paid them back.

—MICHAEL COLLINS on Bloody Sunday killing of British spies, 1920

We have no hopes from English justice. The English call themselves just and in their private dealings they have, or had, some claim to that title. But if said of their public polity, it is an idle boast.

—THOMAS DAVIS, *English Justice*

I think the only true solution of the land question is the abolition of landlordism. The land of Ireland belongs to the people of Ireland.

—JOHN DEVOY (1842-1928), 1878

It's the most important sentence I ever wrote.

—EAMONN MCCANN, on writing
YOU ARE NOW ENTERING FREE DERRY

It is not those who can inflict the most, but those who can suffer most that the victory is certain.

—TERENCE MACSWINEY (1879-1920),
Mayor of Cork and hunger striker, 1920

If we do nothing else we shall rid Ireland of three bad poets.

—PADRAIC PEARSE, prior to 1916 Rising, about
himself, McDonough, and Plunkett

Strength in our hands, truth on our lips, and cleanness in our hearts.

—Motto of the ancient Fianna,
forerunners of the Fenians

Oh God IS THERE A LIFE BEFORE DEATH?

—writing on an Ulster wall

...and only the unfree can know what freedom is.

—SEAN O'RIORDAIN (1916–1977), "Lack of Freedom"

The one great principle of any settlement of the Irish question must be the recognition of the divine right of Irish men, and Irish men alone, to rule Ireland.

—JOHN REDMOND (1856-1918), speech in Chicago
August 18, 1886

When my country takes her place among the nations of the world, then and not until then, let my epitaph be written.

—ROBERT EMMETT's epitaph (died 1803)

I defy anyone to study Irish history without getting a dislike and distrust of England.

—LADY GREGORY (1852-1932)

Burn everything English except their coal.

—JONATHON SWIFT, 1720, in retaliation against British trade barriers

MICHAEL: "Are you lonely going the roads, ma'am?"

OLD WOMAN: "I have my thoughts and I have my hopes."

MICHAEL: "What hopes have you to hold to?"

OLD WOMAN: The hope of getting my beautiful fields back again;

The hope of putting the strangers out of my house."

—WILLIAM BUTLER YEATS, "Deirdre"

Irishmen and Irishwomen; In the name of God and of dead generations from which she receives her old tradition of nationhood, Ireland, through us summons her children to her flag and strikes for her freedom.

—PROCLAMATION OF THE PROVISIONAL GOVERNMENT OF
THE IRISH REPUBLIC, Padraic Pearse, 1916

Our hope and strength, we find at last, is in *ourselves alone.*

—JOHN O'HAGAN (1822-1890), poem in *The Nation*
(Sinn Fein is Gaelic for ourselves alone)

# Irish-Americans

....The last night as we approached Ireland (on the ship, *Nieuw Amsterdam*), there was fog and consequentially thoughts of immortality...

—J. F. POWERS, "Letters From Ireland," 1951-1963

Nobody sees a flower—really—it is so small it takes time—we haven't time—and to see takes time, like to have a friend takes time.

—GEORGIA O'KEEFFE (1887-1986)

A bore is someone who opens his mouth and puts his feats in it.

—HENRY FORD (1863-1947)

Mothers all want their sons to grow up to be president, but they don't want them to become politicians in the process.

—JOHN F. KENNEDY (1917-1963)

No man is an Ireland.

—Chicago mayor RICHARD DALEY (1902-1976)

For the Irish, an ancient people thrust into a grave social struggle in the nineteenth century, the movement from rural to urban life was a transforming experience.

—DENNIS CLARK, *The Irish in Philadelphia*, 1973

We are confronted with insurmountable opportunities.

—WALT KELLY (1913-1973), Pogo

But Jesus, when you don't have any money, the problem is food. When you do have money, it's sex. When you have both, it's health, you worry about getting ruptured or something. If everything is simply jake then you're frightened of death.

—J. P. DUNLEAVY (1926- ), The Ginger Man

Always get married early in the morning. That way, if it doesn't work out you haven't wasted the entire day.

—MICKEY ROONEY (1920- )

You can do anything if you have the enthusiasm. Enthusiasm is the yeast that makes your hopes rise to the sky.

—HENRY FORD

No country in the world, in the history of the world, has endured the hemorrhage which this island endured for a period of a few years for so many of its sons and daughters. These sons and daughters are scattered throughout the world and they give this small Island a family of millions upon millions…in a sense all of them who visit Ireland come Home.

—JOHN F. KENNEDY

Bless you and yours like the Gold of the sun;
Like the Stars of the night / Like the light
    of day
May the luck of the Irish shine bright on
    your way.

—A BLESSING FROM KELLY THE BOY'S COLLECTION

The actual Irish weather report is really a recording made in 1922, which no one has had the occasion to change. "Scattered showers, periods of sunshine."

—WILFID SHEED, *New York Times*, 1971

What's the sense of being Irish if you don't know the world is going to break your heart?

—DANIEL MOYNIHAN (1927-2004)

But look, I was born here. My children were born here. What the hell else do I have to do to be called American?

—JOSEPH P. KENNEDY (1888-1969)

Little old ladies of both sexes, why do I let them bother me?

—JOHN O'HARA (1905-1970)

I hate flowers. I only paint them because they are cheaper than models and they don't move.

—Georgia O'Keeffe

There are several sorts of power working in the fabric of this republic: Water power, steam power and Irish power. The last works hardest of all.

—An observer of 19th century America

Reader, if you have never seen a starving human being, may you never. In my childhood I had been scared with stories of ghosts, and had seen actual skeletons, but imagination had come short of the sight of this man...emaciated to the last degree.

—Asenath Hatch Nicholson (1792-? ),
*Annals of the Famine*

# Irish Music and Dance

God is good but don't dance in a currach.

Irish music is not merely not European, it is quite remote from it. It is, indeed, closer to forms of oriental music.

—SEAN O RIADA (1931–1971)

Dancing is the thing which leads to bad thoughts and evil actions...it is dancing that excites the desires of the body...

—DONAL O'COLMAIN, parish priest, 1670

It would be true to say that over the period 1900 to 1950 most of the important developments in the field of Irish music that did happen took place in the USA.

—SEAMUS MAC MATHUNA, 1987

The older the fiddle, the sweeter the tune.

—PROVERB

From the end of the 18th century dancing at wakes was another familiar sight. The mourners would follow each other in a ring around the coffin to the music of a bagpipe.

—ARTHUR FLYNN, *Irish Dance*, 1998

I'm not here to grieve for your bones or the earth where they're lying, You've company round you of neighbours and friends from this place; The men and women who danced to your music are with you, United you lie in the intimate rhythm of clay.

—MICHAEL COADY (1939- ),
"Stopping by a Clare Graveyard After Hours"

Oh, well do I remember the bleak December day
The landlord and the sheriff came to drive us
	all away
They set my roof on fire with their cursed
	English spleen
And that's the reason why I left old Skibbereen.

—"OLD SKIBBEREEN" (a ballad)

Night is darkest just before the dawn
From dissensions Ireland is reborn.

—F. O'DONOVAN, "On the One Road" (song)

Freddie danced at the ceili in Ardmore almost every night and it was particularly noticeable that the nights he was seen heading towards the hall, a big crowd would follow.

—On dance wizard FREDDIE MURRAY, from *Aspects in the History of Irish Dancing* by Dr. John Cullinane

The harp that once through Tara's halls,
The soul of music shed
Now hangs as mute on Tara's walls,
As if that soul were fled
So sleeps the pride of former days.

—THOMAS MOORE, "The Harp That Once Through
Tara's Halls"

Here is the way to caper / and here is the way
to dance
I came all the way from Ballinagh / To teach you
all to dance.

—A DANCE TEACHER from Cavan in
*The Story of Irish Dance* by Helen Brennan

Birds sing your requiem
While by yon rippling stream
Softly you sleep and dream.
Eileen Aroon!

—CARROL O'DALY, "Eileen Aroon"

All praise to St. Patrick
Who brought to our mountains
The gift of God's faith
The sweet light of His love.

—"Hail to Glorious St. Patrick" (hymn)

The spectacular and difficult dances for the few were cultivated to the neglect of the simple ones for the many.

—P. DE ROISTE, on the revival of Irish dance, 1927

'Tis the last rose of summer, left blooming alone;
All her lovely companions are failed and gone.

—THOMAS MOORE, "The Last Rose of Summer"

Our absentee landlords have left us,
In London they cut a great dash,
While their tenants at home in poor Ireland
Must pay them the rent in hard cash.

—Street ballad of the early 1800s

How do you play the accordion? With a penknife!

—attributed to CHRISTY MOORE

Nobody, unless one who has seen and also *felt* it, can conceive the inexplicable exhilaration of the heart which a dance communicates to the peasantry of Ireland.

—FRANCIS O'NEILL, *Irish Minstrels and Musicians* (1913)

I knew some well in traditional singing until their success prompted them to take lessons in voice production from common modern teachers in towns, and they never could sing Irish any more.

—DR. RICHARD HENEBRY, *Handbook of Irish Music*
(1928)

# Ah, The Humour Is On Me Now

I have never liked working. To me a job is an invasion of privacy.

—DANNY MCGOORTY (1901-1970), Irish pool player

In order to find his equal, an Irishman is forced to talk to God.

—STEPHEN (David O'Hara), *Braveheart*, 1995

Every St. Patrick's Day every Irishman goes out to find another Irishman to make a speech to.

—SHANE LESLIE (1885-1971)

What would a bald headed SOB know about hair lashing across his eyeballs?

—MAUREEN O'HARA castigating director John Ford after a hurtful wind tunnel test

In Ireland the inevitable never happens and the unexpected constantly occurs.

—SIR JOHN PENTLAND MAHAFFY, Provost of Trinity College

The Irish are a fair people; they never speak well of one another.

—SAMUEL JOHNSON (1709-1784)

My one claim to originality among Irishmen is that I never made a speech.

—GEORGE MOORE (1852–1933)

No patty fingers if you please. The proprieties at all times.

—MICHAELEEN FLYNN (Barry Fitzgerald),
*The Quiet Man*, 1952

Have the good manners not to hit the man until he's your husband and entitled to hit you back.

—MICHAELEEN FLYNN (Barry Fitzgerald),
*The Quiet Man*, 1952

Sex never came to Ireland until Teilifís Eireann (Irish television) went on the air.

—OLIVER J. FLANAGAN, Fine Gael TD, 1966

It's the first drop that destroys you, there's no harm at all in the last.

—PROVERB

PAT: "He was an Anglo-Irishman."
MEG: "In the blessed name of God, what's that?"
PAT: "A Protestant with a horse."

—BRENDAN BEHAN, *The Hostage* (1958)

Drink is the curse of the land. It makes you fight with your neighbor. It makes you shoot at your landlord and it makes you miss him.

—OLD SAYING from early days of Temperance league

Marriages are all happy; it's having breakfast together that causes all the trouble.

—PROVERB

Three keys that unlock thoughts: drunkenness, trustfulness and love.

—OLD IRISH TRIAD

Women keep their tongue in their pocket until they marry.

—PROVERB

Twenty years agrowing; twenty years at rest; Twenty years declining; and twenty years when it Doesn't matter whether you're there or not.

—PROVERB

FIRST WOMAN: "The weather can't make its mind up. One minute it's teeming with rain, The next the sun is splitting the trees."

SECOND WOMAN: "I know. You wouldn't know what to pawn, would you?"

—TWO WOMEN IN BELFAST

SUFFRAGETTE: "Well, what is the difference between a man and a woman?"

"I can't conceive," he instantly replied.

—JOHN PENTLAND MAHAFFAY (the Provost of Trinity College) accosted by a suffragette

A literary movement: five or six people who live in the same town and hate each other.

—WILLIAM GEORGE (A. E.) RUSSELL (1867–1935)

I went to the town / Old Lishtowel for a few drinks, and there I met a Knockamore woman with red hair / and gamey eye. I made bold...

—BRENDAN KENNELLY (1936– ), "Moloney Up and At It"

The world famous Abbey Theatre in Dublin was originally the City Morgue. Frank O'Connor once remarked that it had been "fully restored to its original purpose."

DUDE: "I think the clock is fast."
PANTALOON: "Of course it is. It's the fastest clock in these parts."

—JACK B. YEATS (1871–1935),
*The Wonderful Travelers*

If you can see the mountains, it's going to rain, and if you can't see them then it's raining.

—FOLKLORE ABOUT MOUNT GABRIEL IN WEST CORK

May God increase your neighbors—those of them that are useful to you.

—BLESSING

# More Pearls From The Emerald Isle

No man ever wore a scarf as warm as his daughter's arm around his neck.

—FOLKLORE

I felt it like a torchlight procession going down my throat.

—JOHN LOUIS O'SULLIVAN (1813-1895)

Irishness is not primarily a question of birth or blood or language. It is the condition of being involved in the Irish situation, and usually of being mauled by it.

—CONOR CRUISE O'BRIEN (1917– )

SO YOU MARRIED SOMEONE ELSE BEHIND MY BACK! YOU MAY CONSIDER OUR ENGAGEMENT DEFINITELY AT AN END, YOU SHANTY IRISH CREEP!

—Author PEGGY RYAN to a friend with whom she had an understanding, 1932

English is a world language and we are lucky to have it, particularly as we have embroidered it with tweedy fol-de-lols and porter stains which are unmistakably Irish and proud of it.

—MYLES NA GCOPALEEN (Flann O'Brien)

For the Great Gaels of Ireland / Are the men
that God made mad
For all their wars are merry / And all their songs
are sad.

—G. K. CHESTERTON (1874-1936)

The hospitality of an Irishman is not the running account of posted and ledgered courtesies, as in other countries; it springs, like all his qualities, his faults, his virtues, directly from his heart.

—DANIEL O'CONNELL

Perhaps we are not meant to know some things, for that is life too. A seeking. It may be our only purpose here.

—GABRIEL BYRNE (1960- )

I do not know what the custom of the English may be, but it is the custom of the Irish to hate villains.

—MARY SHELLEY (1797–1851), *Frankenstein*

We had this idea of Ireland rammed down our throats. So we threw it up.

—BONO (1960– )

When anyone asks me about the Irish character, I say look at the trees, maimed, stark and misshapen, but ferociously tenacious.

—EDNA O'BRIEN

In England you can say anything as long as you do the right thing. In Ireland you can do anything as long as you say the right thing.

—EAMON DE VALERA

Three things best for a chief: Justice, peace, and an army.

—OLD IRISH TRIAD

Nothing is politically correct which is morally wrong.

—DANIEL O'CONNELL

The English and the American dislike only some Irish—the same Irish that the Irish themselves detest, Irish writers—the ones that think.

—BRENDAN BEHAN

It has always been very curious to me how Irish sentiment sticks in this half-way house—how it continues to apparently hate the English and at the same time continues to imitate them.

—DOUGLAS HYDE, lecture in Leinster Hall,<br/>January 25, 1892

The well-fed does not understand the lean.

—PROVERB

Women do not drink liquor but it disappears when they are present.

—PROVERB

I go out there so I can look into myself, and when I'm there I can see myself standing still and the rest of the world going mad.

—DES LAVELLE, on the Skellig Islands

O stranger pause when passing by
As you are now so once was I
As I am now so you shall be
So be prepared to follow me.

—GRAVE INSCRIPTION

I promise to abstain from all intoxicating drinks, except used medicinally and by order of a medical man, and to discountenance the cause and practice of intemperance.

—Fr. Mathew's Total Abstinence Society
pledge, 1838

Teetotalism has taken from the people their only enjoyment. They are altogether without public amusement.

—The Nation's (newspaper) response to
Fr. Mathews temperance crusade

Would to God that this (blood) was shed for Ireland.

—Attributed to Patrick Sarsfield, as his last words
fighting in exile for France

We huddled together like sheep for sale at the marketplace of Strabane.

—PATRICK MCGILL OF GLENTIES, on memories of the Hiring Fair when he was 12

# Closing

In closing, here are a toast and two Irish Blessings: one, humorous; the other, famous.

Patrick was a gentleman; / Through strategy and
    strength
He drove the snakes from Erin. / A toast then to
    his health
But not too many toasts then / Or you'll lose
    your sense and then
You'll see those snakes again.

May those that love us, love us
And those that don't love us,
May God turn their hearts
And if He doesn't turn their hearts,
May He turn their ankles
So we will know them by their limping.

—HUMOROUS IRISH BLESSING

May the road rise to meet you
May the wind be always at your back
May the sun shine warm upon your face
And the rain fall soft upon your fields
And until we meet again
May God hold you in the palm of his hand.

—FAMOUS IRISH BLESSING